OYCE MARÍA MAGDALENA CAMPOS-PONS
MID KAMALA IBRAHIM ISHAG ROSEMARY
ERRY JAMES MARSHALL ZANELE MUHOLI M
EMEKA OGBOH TOYIN OJIH ODUTOLA ZIZIP
SHERALD YINKA SHONIBARE CARRIE MAE
LARRY ACHIAMPONG EL ANATSUI SONIA
CAVE JOANA CHOUMALI LUBAINA HIMID K
ULAYE KONATÉ IBRAHIM MAHAMA KERRY
.N. ODUNDO HAROLD OFFEH CHRIS OFILI I
WA FAITH RINGGOLD ATHI-PATRA RUGA A
WEEMS KEHINDE WILEY LYNETTE YIADOM

OYCE MARÍA MAGDALENA CAMPOS-PONS
MID KAMALA IBRAHIM ISHAG ROSEMARY K
ERRY JAMES MARSHALL ZANELE MUHOLI M
EMEKA OGBOH TOYIN OJIH ODUTOLA ZIZIP
SHERALD YINKA SHONIBARE CARRIE MAE
LARRY ACHIAMPONG EL ANATSUI SONIA
CAVE JOANA CHOUMALI LUBAINA HIMID K
ULAYE KONATÉ IBRAHIM MAHAMA KERRY
.N. ODUNDO HAROLD OFFEH CHRIS OFILI I
WA FAITH RINGGOLD ATHI-PATRA RUGA A
WEEMS KEHINDE WILEY LYNETTE YIADOM

BLACK ARTISTS SHAPING THE WORLD

12/21

BLACK ARTISTS SHAPING THE WORLD

BY SHARNA JACKSON

Consultant Dr Zoé Whitley

CONTENTS

INTRODUCTION

Black Artists Shaping the World is a celebration! It's a party to praise some of the many talented Black artists creating exciting and important work today. This book is your invitation to join in. Here, you'll meet the artists, and discover how their art shapes and shares their opinions of the world.

Some of our artists are already famous, some you may not have heard of yet, but all of them are brilliant at making us look and think about art and life. They work in many different ways, and explore all kinds of ideas. Their gifts shape our world, too.

This book is not primarily about race and racism, but it is a fact that throughout history Black people have been treated unequally, and Black artists have often been denied the recognition they deserve. This book is a contribution to change.

I've used "Black" with a capital "B" to describe artists and people from a variety of backgrounds—those who were born and live in Africa, and those from the African diaspora. "Black" is a term that was first used positively in the United States by African American civil rights activists who wanted to assert their identity and show pride in their African ancestry.

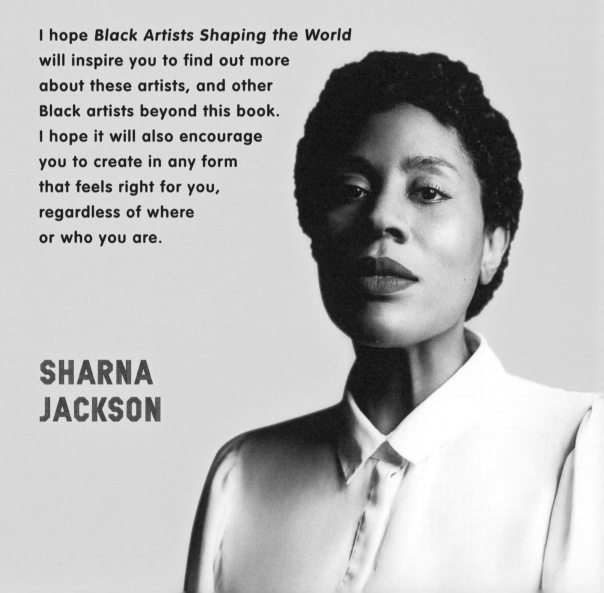

It was very difficult to choose just twenty-six artists.
Dr Zoé Whitley and I thought about the many practices—
photography, painting, performance, ceramics, textiles
and installations, and everything in between—and selected
some of the very best artists working with these art forms.

I hope *Black Artists Shaping the World*
will inspire you to find out more
about these artists, and other
Black artists beyond this book.
I hope it will also encourage
you to create in any form
that feels right for you,
regardless of where
or who you are.

SHARNA
JACKSON

LARRY
ACHIAMPONG

"Sankofa!" This is a saying that Larry Achiampong's mother used regularly when he was growing up in East London. A Ghanaian Twi word, it roughly means "go back and get it." Fascinated by the notion of moving backward and forward through time, Larry developed "Sanko-time"—an idea that someone can use the past to prepare for the future. Larry's concept is at the core of *Relic Traveller*—a world-building, fictional project that began in 2017 and carries on today.

In Larry's rich and detailed future, Western nations have collapsed but fifty-four African countries—which joined together to form a Pan-African Union—have survived and are thriving. To ensure they learn lessons from how nations governed in the past, the Union's Relic Travellers' Alliance sends explorers with space-travel tech across the world to collect clues and gather stories. The travelers are specifically seeking testimonies from people from the African diaspora who had been oppressed and exploited. These stories are part of a healing process for the Union. They are also used to create a new way of governing by listening to "the people," rather than "the politicians."

Larry uses different media to their strengths to express his message. *Relic Traveller* therefore exists in many forms—as short films, music scores, installations, performances and flags. He has also used the colors and patterns from his flags to replace the traditional red, white and blue on the signs that display the name of Westminster Station on the London Underground.

RELIC TRAVELLER

In this ongoing work, Larry Achiampong imagines a strong Pan-African Union, whose wish and responsibility is to form a fair future for the planet.

Flags from many Western countries also feature red, white and blue. The four flags in *Relic Traveller* intentionally do not. Each flag includes fifty-four stars, one for each African country. The use of black represents the people in the Union. Red signifies their blood and struggles. Green reflects the lands—the plant life and environmental resources. Yellow promises prosperity and a bright future. Larry's flags have been flown in public, internationally, and this is important to him. Larry does not want his work only to be shown in museums and galleries, as he knows that not everyone feels welcome there— a serious issue that art spaces must address. He wants as many people as possible to see his work, and to feel connected to it.

A Pan-African flag for the Relic Travellers' Alliance, in black, red, green and yellow

EL ANATSUI

El Anatsui was born in Ghana, but lives and works in Nigeria. In 2007, he made a huge, glistening, undulating wall hanging called *Bleeding Takari II*. It has red parts that look like blood which has soaked into the artwork, and is now dripping onto the floor. This might seem brutal, but it doesn't necessarily mean that something has been broken or destroyed. El believes that blood can also mean rebirth, or growth.

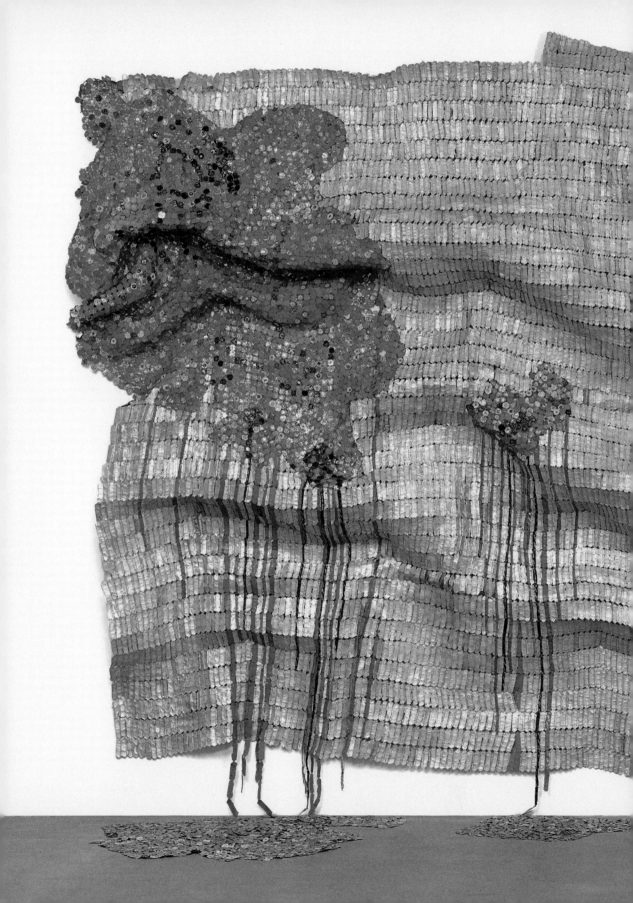

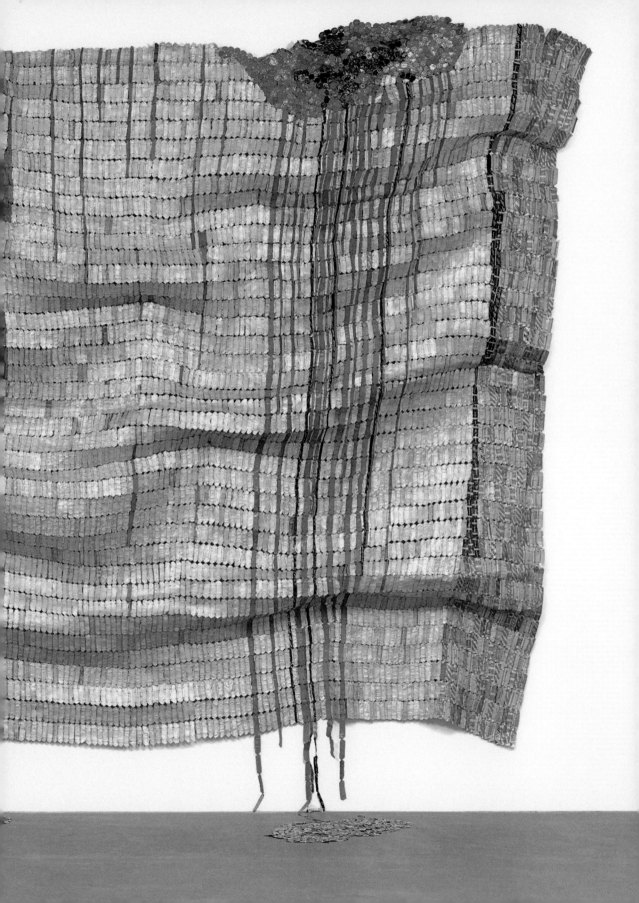

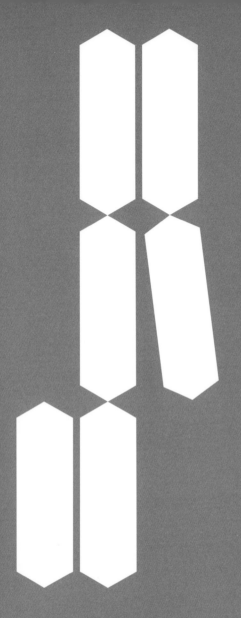

BLEEDING TAKARI II

In this work, the blood might be from anyone or anything.
"Takari" is a made-up word that El Anatsui uses to mean
"any thing, person, object, country or continent."

In the late 1990s, El found a big bag of bottle caps in a bush, where they had been discarded by liquor distilleries. Investigating them closely, he wondered if something as rigid as metal could be transformed into something fluid. He had the idea of linking the caps together with copper wire. In this way, he did more than simply recycle the caps; he gave them a new life, and new meaning.

In his studio—sometimes with as many as forty assistants— he works with the caps in small batches, which he calls "blocks." Once these blocks are arranged into larger pieces, El spends time with them, over many days, moving them and carefully looking at them until he is happy with the overall shape. When the work is finished and ready to display, El does not give museums strict rules on how to hang it. He allows it to be displayed in any way. This allows the museum also to be a part of the work—and El can discover even more about it himself.

El thinks a lot about people. He thinks about the people who made the caps, and who drank from the liquor bottles. He thinks about his assistants who shape the caps, and of course he thinks about himself. By considering humanity, he believes there is something spiritual in his works.

But El's art is not just spiritual, and it's not just about transforming everyday objects. His work is informed by the slave trade that tied Africa with Europe and the Americas. Liquor was one of the things that Europeans wanted to exchange for goods—and eventually people—in Africa.

SONIA BOYCE

Sonia Boyce is a British artist who works with a huge variety of media—painting, printmaking, filmmaking, drawing, sound, photography, and more. In 1987, she created a large photo-based work with a long title. In full, it is *From Tarzan to Rambo: English Born "Native" Considers her Relationship to the Constructed/Self Image and her Roots in Reconstruction*. In her work, Sonia is the *English Born "Native"*; her *Roots* are her African heritage. When she made the work, she was thinking about how Black people are represented in the media we watch and read—and what that means.

Sonia started by looking at media from the 1940s and '50s—images
she saw as a child—and media from the 1980s, when she made the
work. *Tarzan*, a white character first created in 1912, has appeared
in many comics and films. He is known as "The King of the Jungle."
In his stories, he is shown as strong and brave. In comparison,
the African people are shown as primitive and inarticulate.
On the left, there is an image Sonia took from a comic, in which

the Africans say "the buzzing bird sends us a victim." In the original comic, they were looking up at a plane in the sky. They called it a "buzzing bird," because they were represented as simple and unable to understand the world. White men were the masters of the "wild"—even though it was the "natives" who came from there. Tarzan himself appears in Sonia's work, to the left of the comic. He is almost invisible, but his pose is still powerful.

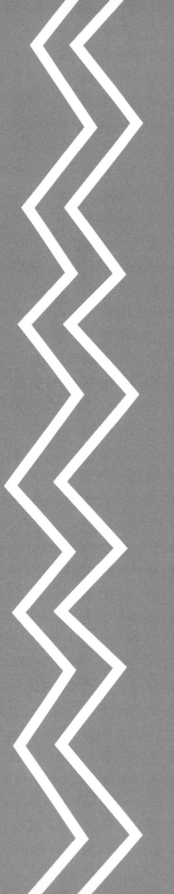

FROM TARZAN TO RAMBO: ENGLISH BORN "NATIVE" CONSIDERS HER RELATIONSHIP TO THE CONSTRUCTED/SELF IMAGE AND HER ROOTS IN RECONSTRUCTION

Sonia Boyce's artwork shows stereotypes created by white people to enable them to laugh at Black bodies. In her work, she questions how we see ourselves, how others see us, who creates these images—and why.

Sonia's work is about the media. It resembles an actual film strip, with its widescreen format and repeated images. In the twelve photo booth portraits of Sonia, she is recreating some of the stereotypes she saw when she was younger. She is making facial expressions that were seen in "voodoo trances," where people are under a spell. This was a common representation of Black people in the past, as was the child with wide white eyes on the left of the work. This image was very popular—and very racist—and appeared on television, advertisements and packaging.

These representations were so common and powerful that, as a child, Sonia thought they really showed what Black people were like. Her work was therefore not just about white people's thoughts about Black people, but Black people's thoughts about themselves, too.

The left side of this work—in black and white—is a reference to how Black people were shown in classic Hollywood films and in older media. Sonia drew over the photos on the bottom row to make them look more like comic book images. The work is divided by a photocopy of an African scarf, referencing Black women who traditionally have worn these fabrics. The right side—in color—is the *Reconstruction* Sonia mentions in the title. Now her dark skin and wide white eyes appear between real leaves that were sewn onto the canvas. She is referencing the false idea that African countries were just "jungle," and not modern nations.

Rambo is also mentioned in Sonia's title. He was a popular film character in the 1980s. Like Tarzan, he is a white "hero" who has adventures in a jungle. Sonia noticed many similarities between the two characters, even though they were created many decades apart. She noticed Rambo was essentially Tarzan, reconstructed.

MARÍA MAGDALENA CAMPOS-PONS

In 2013, María Magdalena Campos-Pons created an installation for the Cuban pavilion at the Venice Biennale—the world's oldest international art exhibition, which takes place in Italy every two years. She collaborated on the project with her husband, Neil Leonard, a composer. Titled *53+1=54+1=55. Letter of the Year*, the installation was a multimedia experience formed of videos, sounds and sculptures. It included many birdcages, and inside them were small screens. These screens showed Cubans imagining they were talking to family members who lived elsewhere. As the participants shared their daily lives, the videos demonstrated how powerful it would be for the people to reconnect with their relatives.

Birdcages are basically traps that keep things in—but they also keep things out. Magda (as she is known) and Neil's installation was about staying, leaving and loss, and how we think about these things. They are at the core of Magda's work. She has Nigerian, Chinese and Hispanic heritage. She now lives in the United States, but she was born in Matanzas, Cuba. There, she grew up on a sugar plantation. Her African ancestors were enslaved workers on sugar plantations, while her Chinese ancestors were servants in sugar mills. Magda calls upon their spirits for this work, thinking about migration and moving, sharing her diverse background.

On the opening evening of her installation in Venice, without warning or announcement, Magda put on a performance. She led a parade of musicians from Cuba and Scotland, inspired by the Abakuá, an Afro-Cuban secret society. Magda wore what you see in *The Flag. Color Code Venice 13*—a fusion of Spanish, Afro-Caribbean and Chinese clothing, a combination of her cultures. Her robe is Chinese. The ribbons in her hand signify the distances between Matanzas in Cuba, Ife in Nigeria (her great-grandparents' homeland) and Boston in the U.S. (where she lived at the time). The birdcages on her head and in her hand show how Magda manages to balance her blended background.

THE FLAG. COLOR CODE VENICE 13

This Polaroid work, created by María Magdalena Campos-Pons, is a sort of souvenir of the multimedia installation and performance she made in Venice, Italy, in 2013.

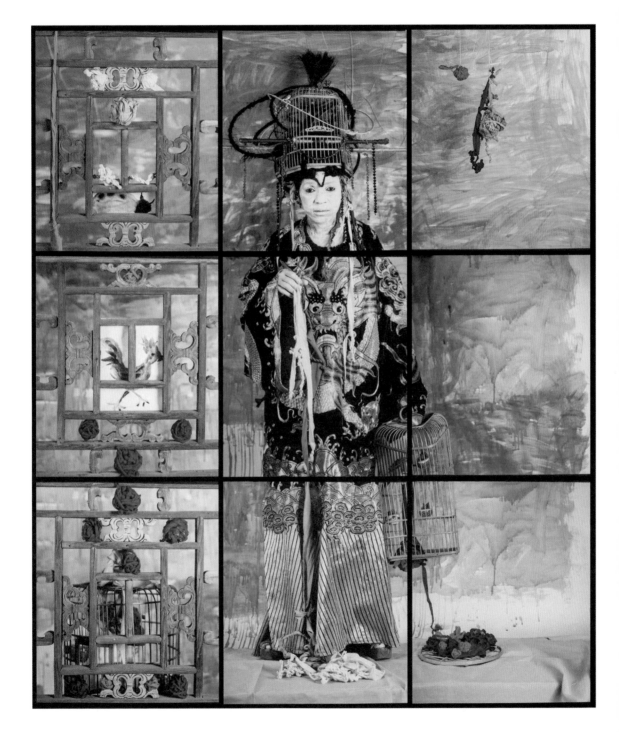

In 1991, a terrible event happened when a young Black man named Rodney King was brutally beaten by members of the Los Angeles Police Department, leading to riots in the city in 1992. Since 1992, the African American artist Nick Cave has created over five hundred "Soundsuits"— a unique, colorful series of wearable sculptures. The connection between the dates—and between Rodney King and Nick Cave—is not a coincidence. The attack on King had a profound effect on Nick, and on his work.

In response to King's beating, Nick said: "I started thinking about myself more and more as a Black man—as someone who was discarded, devalued, viewed as less than…"
He thought about how visible and vulnerable Black bodies are in society. He decided to create a suit of armor out of twigs, as a type of protection. The twigs, strung together with fine wire, made a noise as he moved. The first "Soundsuit" was born.

Every suit is made by hand from a wide range of materials, including fake fur and feathers, buttons and beads, dolls and doilies. When Nick finds something soundsuit-able, he spends time figuring out where each piece fits. Once he is happy with the overall design, he reveals his new Soundsuit to the world.

The Soundsuits are a sort of contradiction. They make people look … but they hide the wearer. On the inside, they are safe, private places … but, seen from the outside, they are larger than life and take up space.

Soundsuits are not just playful costumes. They celebrate African and African American traditions, Mardi Gras parades and rituals. People can wear them, but they can also perform in them—to music, dancing and drumming from crowds. When Soundsuits are worn by troupes of dancers and musicians, they give everyone a sense of what it might feel like to be free—free from being judged, and free from judging others.

The Soundsuits made by Nick Cave hide race, gender, class—everything about the wearer. You don't know who is inside a Soundsuit; you only see the artwork.

SOUNDSUIT

JOANA CHOUMALI

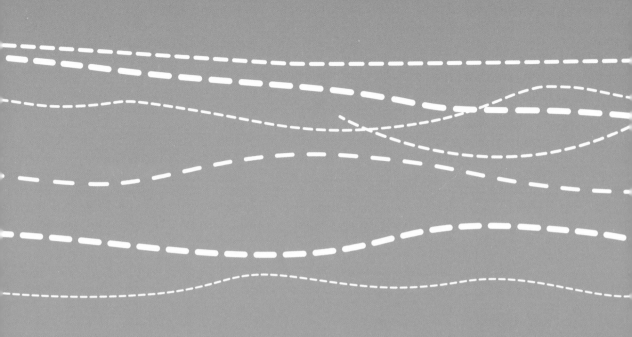

Every morning, between the early hours of five and seven, Joana Choumali walks around Abidjan in Côte d'Ivoire. While her family are asleep, she captures the city with her cameras. With her DSLR, she surveys her surroundings, looking at landscapes and buildings. With her smartphone, she snaps the people she sees on the streets—the early risers and the latecomers. When the city is quiet, its true beauty is revealed.

Early morning is a magical time for Joana.
It sits between night and day, between past and present, between dreams and reality. The work shown here, *Because We Actually Played Outside As Kids*, was made in 2020, and is part of a series called *Alba'hian*. This word means "the first light of the day" in the Agni language. It describes the feelings that arrive with the start of a new day. Joana wants to evoke all of this energy in her work—which is photography, adorned with embroidery.

When the sun has fully risen, Joana returns to her studio and begins to create her images. She prints her photographs directly onto her canvas, then adds layers of sheer fabric to recreate the light of dawn and the dreamy morning fog. She adds gold paints, and then begins to sew in vivid-colored threads, weaving her feelings into her work.

This is almost like meditation for Joana, with each stitch a mark of her emotions. Photographs are instant, but she works on her sewing slowly, and each piece can take months to make. It is a process in which Joana is patient, and takes her time to discover the direction of the final piece. When she begins, she does not know how a work will end. She does not design, or plan, or choose the colors first. She lets her photographs give her guidance, and she lets her imagination roam free.

Through making her dreamy embroidered photographs, Joana Choumali has discovered the beauty, poetry and energy that are right on her doorstep.

BECAUSE WE ACTUALLY
PLAYED OUTSIDE AS KIDS

LUBAINA HIMID

Lubaina Himid was born in Zanzibar, and moved to England as a baby. When visiting museums in Europe, she began to notice something about the grand paintings of rich old families that hang in such galleries. She saw that Black people—if present—were almost always enslaved workers or servants. They would be at the edge, by the picture frame, holding onto horses, trays or teapots, but they were never at the center. Their role in the paintings was only to boost the appearance and power of their masters. There was nothing about *them* in the portraits—only what they *did* for the white people who owned them. Lubaina wanted to bring the slaves and servants together, to tell their untold stories. She wanted to take them out of the paintings, away from their masters. She wanted to give them names, bodies, and lives.

In her installation *Naming the Money* from 2004, Lubaina created one hundred life-size painted cutouts, which stand upright in the gallery. On their back, in a short poem written on a sales invoice, each person tells you their real name, followed by a convenient name given to them by their masters. They tell you what they used to do—and what they're forced into doing now. Then, they tell you something that shows they are being positive, and making the most of their horrific situation.

> My name is Asiza
> They call me Sally
> I loved to work the clay
> Now I sweep the yard
> But I love mud

The one hundred plywood people share ten professions. They are either painters, ceramicists, map makers, shoe makers, dancers, drummers, viola da gamba players, toy makers, herbalists or dog trainers. The figures are arranged in groups, so that they can talk, think and remember with each other—and possibly plan for the future.

When Lubaina was first working on this installation, her idea was to create a series of ten portraits called *Gifts to Kings*. However, while making the work, she realized that this title gave away the power of the people in her portraits. As "gifts," they once again became objects. Through Lubaina's new title and format, the work became less about objects and more about naming. She gave the people their power back.

My name is Effiong
They call me John
I used to make rings for royal fingers
Now I make shoes for ladies' feet
But I have the gold

A soundtrack plays over *Naming the Money*, featuring music from
all over the world and Lubaina Himid narrating the poems she wrote
for the installation. Each of her people has finally been given a voice.

KAMALA IBRAHIM ISHAG

Kamala Ibrahim Ishag has been called "the first modern woman painter in Sudan." She is an innovator and an icon. Born in Omdurman in 1939, she began her studies at the College of Fine Arts at the Khartoum Technical Institute. She was one of the very first women to go there. In 1960, along with two other painters, she started a new art movement, known as the Khartoum School. They used traditional Islamic imagery and simplified Arabic writing in their work, which was rare and fresh then. It was also important: Sudan had just become an independent country, no longer under British and Egyptian rule, so this was the perfect time to create a new visual language. The Khartoum School was extremely influential, and the reputation for modern painting in Sudan grew.

After graduating, Kamala went to London to study further. She then returned to the Institute to teach. With two of her students, she broke away from the Khartoum School and founded a new movement. Her Crystalist Group wanted to look away from traditional styles and create radically different work. They wanted to be free from just thinking about the physical world and its stifling rules; they wanted to look beyond, into the spiritual realm. This was not a protest—Kamala just wanted to progress and change.

She was particularly intrigued by a ritual called "Zār." Full of music, dancing and incense, this ritual was performed by Sudanese women to rid themselves of demons—but not actual devils, as you might think at first. It was a kind of therapy, to cure minor ailments and to treat aspects of their personality they wanted to change, like rudeness. Zār became a theme in Kamala's work. Contorted, haunted-looking women look out at us from many of her canvases.

Nature is another theme. Kamala believes that nature communicates with us. In *Two Women (Eve and Eve)*, painted in 2016, her figures float in a forest, side by side, perhaps brought together by the forces of nature. Or maybe the women *themselves* are the force, as the trees—with small faces in their trunks—bend towards them. Kamala's process is possibly inspired by nature, too. She paints every day and she works organically, creating directly onto her canvas, never sketching first. As her ideas change, she simply adds or erases parts of her painting.

TWO WOMEN (EVE AND EVE)

Kamala Ibrahim Ishag loves plants, and wants them to be treated gently and protected. She thinks a lot about the relationship between humans and plants. Plants are born, grow, eat and die. Just like us.

ROSEMARY KARUGA

Rosemary Karuga is known as the "mother of East African art." She was born in Kenya in 1928, and attended Saint Theresa's School in Nairobi. There, the nuns in charge nurtured her talent and encouraged her creativity. In 1950, on their recommendation, Rosemary went to Makerere University in Uganda to study design, painting and sculpture. She was the first woman ever to attend its School of Fine Art. While she was a student, she tried to sell her work, but she didn't have a lot of success. So, when she graduated, Rosemary returned to Kenya to be an art teacher in the countryside—a job that provided a guaranteed income. She got married and had three children. She withdrew from the art world.

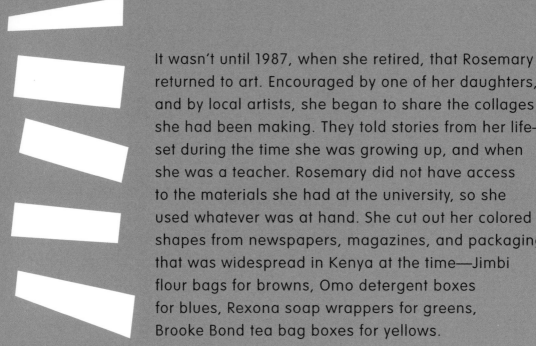

It wasn't until 1987, when she retired, that Rosemary returned to art. Encouraged by one of her daughters, and by local artists, she began to share the collages she had been making. They told stories from her life— set during the time she was growing up, and when she was a teacher. Rosemary did not have access to the materials she had at the university, so she used whatever was at hand. She cut out her colored shapes from newspapers, magazines, and packaging that was widespread in Kenya at the time—Jimbi flour bags for browns, Omo detergent boxes for blues, Rexona soap wrappers for greens, Brooke Bond tea bag boxes for yellows.

At sixty years old, resourceful and resilient, Rosemary finally became a full-time artist. For four months, she was an artist-in-residence at Paa Ya Paa, a gallery in Nairobi. She was part of a group show, and then had her own solo show. In 1990, she was commissioned to illustrate a new edition of a famous book, *The Palm-Wine Drinkard*, by Amos Tutuola. After it was published, her work became very popular and well-known internationally. Rosemary was included in exhibitions in New York and London. She flew for the very first time to put on a show in Paris. In her later years, she moved to Ireland, where her eyesight became weak and she had to use a hearing aid. Nonetheless, Rosemary remains an inspiration to many.

WOMAN STANDING

Rosemary Karuga's colorful collages show what can be made out of humble materials, such as paper, packaging, scissors and glue.

ABDOULAYE
KONATÉ

Abdoulaye Konaté focuses on fabrics to create his fantastic hanging works. He makes these with the material that surrounds him. Mali, the country where he lives and works, produces a lot of cotton—over 500,000 tons per year. It is therefore widely available to him and to other artists in his country. There is a strong tradition of textile-making in Mali, and so fabrics are very meaningful there.

As a child, Abdoulaye loved to paint, and he later studied in both his native Mali and Cuba. He does not work with paint as much now, though. To Abdoulaye, fabrics function in a better way, because they can reflect his local and cultural histories while also being beautiful.

The small strips that form Abdoulaye's large pieces are inspired by costumes worn by the Senufo musicians of southeastern Mali, and by the Kôrêdugaw ritual of the Segou and Koulikoro regions. Abdoulaye's process is less traditional. He creates designs on his computer first, so he can plan where all the strips will go. Then, women working in the factory next to his studio spin and dye the cotton. Next, his four male assistants sew the intricate works together on the floor. Traditional gendered work roles are reversed.

Color is important to Abdoulaye. Indigo blue is the color of Mali; it features in many of his works, including *Femme du Sahel* (French for "Woman of the Sahel"). He composes the colors himself, so they look exactly right. To get his range of colors, he looks at people—where they live, where they work and where they go—for inspiration. When the work is complete, Abdoulaye stitches his name as a signature.

His art is more than simply beautiful; it also addresses social, political and environmental issues. By working this way with humble fabric, Abdoulaye raises the fabric's value while also raising concerns. He has done this on a massive scale. To comment on the AIDS epidemic, he created a nearly 20,000-square-foot work that was pulled across a soccer field by two hundred people for the opening of the Africa Cup of Nations tournament in 2002.

FEMME DU SAHEL

Abdoulaye Konaté is concerned by many important issues, including global warming. For instance, the Sahel—a vast strip of land that spans Mali, Senegal, Niger and Mauritania—was once grassland, but is quickly turning into a desert.

IBRAHIM
MAHAMA

In Ghana, where Ibrahim Mahama was born and lives, young cobblers—known as "shoeshine boys"—travel from their homes in the quiet countryside into big, busy cities like Accra and Kumasi. There, they seek materials—especially wood—to make boxes to hold their tools, such as hammers and shoe-heels. When they find what they need, they shape the pieces into little house-like structures. Once they are finished, the boys travel across the city. There, they bang their boxes like drums, shouting about their services to attract attention. Then they repair and polish their customers' shoes.

NON-ORIENTABLE NKANSA

The work is named after one of Ibrahim Mahama's collaborators, Nkansa.
He was "non-orientable" because he refused to be persuaded that making
this artwork was a good use of time. To him, it didn't mean or do anything.
Many others have disagreed.

Ibrahim, along with dozens of collaborators (many of them migrant workers who come from rural Ghana, like the shoeshine boys), gathered approximately two thousand of these boxes. Then they made this towering architectural installation, called *Non-Orientable Nkansa*. Created in 2017, it is covered with small stickers and name tags, and filled with the tools that the shoeshine boys used.

Ibrahim is interested in transforming objects that he finds—changing the way they are used, putting them in new places, and therefore giving them new meanings. Ibrahim and his team got their materials by swapping new boxes for the old ones belonging to the boys, or else they made their own. Working with the boxes in this way, Ibrahim was thinking about the worth of the shoeshine boys. He was appreciating the way the boys come to cities and do useful work.

The boxes were made into *Non-Orientable Nkansa* in a former paint factory in Ghana. By putting the boxes together in a sculptural way, Ibrahim is adding more layers to the boxes' histories. Suddenly the boxes are more than "things"; they become "art."

KERRY JAMES MARSHALL

The African American artist Kerry James Marshall
is considered one of the greatest living painters.
He famously uses deep blacks to paint his people,
and he never mixes black into other colors in his work.
Representation is important to Kerry—he is driven
to make sure that Black people are seen in painting
and included in the history of the form.

Kerry's settings include everyday places such as living
rooms, nightclubs, restaurant booths and barber shops.
In *School of Beauty, School of Culture*, painted in 2012,
he opens the door to a "beauty school." Beauty salons often
function as Black community spaces, where the happenings
and conversations around you are just as exciting as your
haircut. There, you not only learn about the business of beauty,
but also transfer traditions and tell tales to each other.
Beauty salons can be safe, sacred spaces.

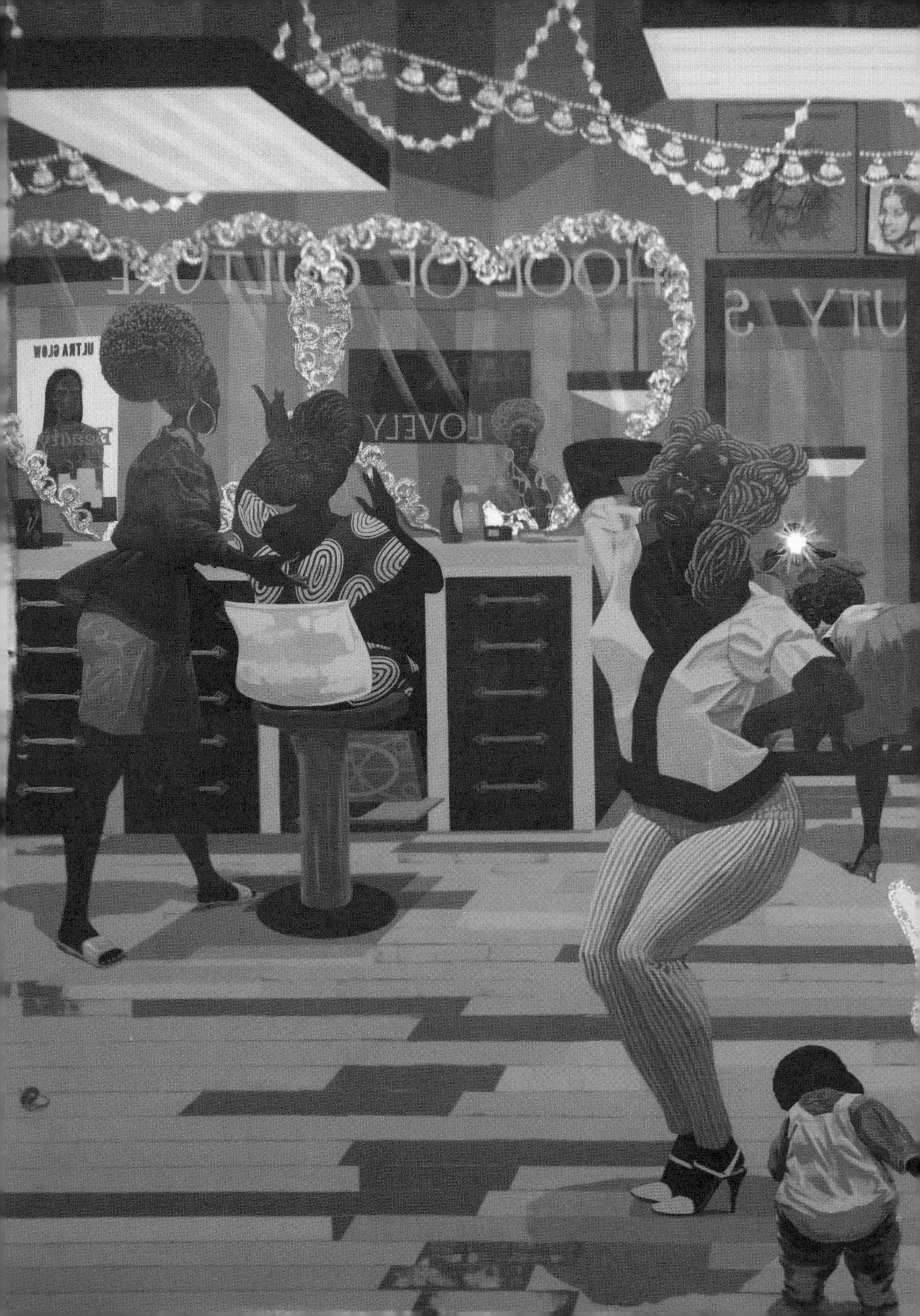
ULTRA GLOW
LOVELY

Hans Holbein the Younger, *Jean de Dinteville and Georges de Selve*
(*"The Ambassadors"*), 1533

SCHOOL OF BEAUTY,
SCHOOL OF CULTURE

**Like Hans Holbein, Kerry James Marshall makes use of black,
red, green and yellow. But, as in the work of Larry Achiampong
(see page 13), these are also the colors of Africa.**

Kerry's painting is rich with references and cultural clues.
It is a celebration of Black beauty, and many elements confirm this. "Black is Beautiful" was a movement started in the 1960s to counteract the racist idea that Black people are ugly—that their hair and features are undesirable. In Kerry's painting, posters on the walls and reflected in the heart-shaped, graduation-photo-adorned mirrors exclaim "dark" and "lovely"—which is also the name of a Black hair-care brand. Kerry's figures are just that—dark and lovely. Also on the wall is a poster for the artist Chris Ofili's 2010 exhibition at Tate Britain in London. Above the door is a signed cover of Lauryn Hill's classic record album, *The Miseducation of Lauryn Hill*. Next to this is an image of Cheryl Lynn Bruce, Kerry's wife.

There are also key references to historic Old Master paintings. In the center is a flash of a camera and a person crouching, taking a photograph. It is possibly Kerry himself, appearing as a small self-portrait within his larger painting. This has echoes of Diego Velázquez's painting, *Las Meninas*, from 1656, and Jan Van Eyck's *Arnolfini Portrait* from 1434.

One curious element at the center of the work draws all of these references together—and only the children at the foreground of the painting seem to notice it. They are gesturing towards an askew image of the blonde-haired, blue-eyed Princess Aurora from Disney's *Sleeping Beauty*. This is a comment on how white beauty standards are everywhere, and how they are attractive to children, even among the Black beauty that surrounds them. The way Aurora's image appears in Kerry's painting is reminiscent of how Hans Holbein used a skull in his 1533 work, "The Ambassadors."

ZANELE
MUHOLI

Zanele Muholi is a visual activist, who uses the pronoun "they," instead of "she" or "he." They also like to be called by their last name. Muholi uses photography to take symbolic ownership of their identity; to remind themselves—and others who have historically been marginalized—that they exist; and to boldly state: we are worthy. In particular, Muholi has worked closely with the Black LGBTQIA+ community—in South Africa, but also globally—for many years.

Muholi's work is often shaped by personal experiences. This self-portrait—*Bester I, Mayotte, 2015*—is perhaps the very best example. It is part of a series called *Somnyama Ngonyama, Hail the Dark Lioness*. "Ngonyama" (or Lioness) is Muholi's mother's clan-name. "Bester" was Muholi's mother's first name. "Mayotte" is the place where Muholi took this photograph, in the year 2015.

Muholi was the youngest of eight children—in isiZulu, Zanele means "enough." When Muholi's father died shortly after Muholi was born, Bester had to work incredibly hard, spending long hours away from her family. She was employed by a white family under apartheid—a brutal system that meant people in South Africa were divided by race and forced to live separately. Bester worked like this for forty-two years.

In the image, Muholi stares down the camera lens, directly at us. Their black skin is rich and deep. At a quick glance, you might think they are wearing simple but bold accessories and clothing. Look again, though, and you will notice that Muholi's earrings and regal crown are clothes pegs. Around their shoulders is a doormat, in place of a shawl. These are not random household objects, or a fashion statement. These are materials that Muholi uses in their photographic work, and they are full of meaning. They are used as symbols of Black African women's experiences throughout history.

BESTER I, MAYOTTE, 2015

This powerful photograph is a tribute to Zanele Muholi's mother, but also to domestic workers across the world. It honors their strength and resilience.

MAGDALENE ODUNDO

Magdalene Odundo has always been interested in creating, but working with ceramics—the form she is most celebrated for—did not come easily at first. She began her career by studying graphics and commercial art, and then worked at an advertising agency in Nairobi, Kenya. In the early 1970s, she moved to the U.K. for further study. There, while attending a course, she encountered clay. For the first eight weeks, Magdalene struggled to understand what the pottery wheel did, or how it worked—but, after twelve weeks, she understood.

Magdalene responded to the clay, and in return the clay responded to her. It gave her answers. It gave her a way to express her inner thoughts, to think about what it means to be human, and to tell the "history of our humanity." After all, people have made pots in every culture, all across the world, since the Stone Age.

Magdalene believes we are all connected to clay. It is one of the first materials we play with as children, squeezing it in our hands, shaping it into little people. People are also Magdalene's main reference, and many of her vessels remind us of this. In her work, we can see the curves of spines and stomachs, of necks and nipples that look like the female form. For Magdalene, the idea that women can contain life makes them the "ultimate vessel." Her works have an inside and an outside, a skin and a body. They capture stances, movements and gestures. The flexibility of the human body reminds Magdalene of clay. When she creates her vessels, she dances with them and she embraces them. Her work embodies bodies.

Magdalene's clay course back in the 1970s changed her life—and it also took her back to Africa for a while. She returned to learn about the way pottery is made in Kenya and Nigeria, and then she went on to New Mexico, China, Japan and India. Always, she loved spending time watching women working by hand with clay.

UNTITLED #15

Magdalene Odundo wants people to be amazed at the power of clay. For her, the fact that this simple material can be formed into absolutely anything is magical.

HAROLD
OFFEH

In 2008, Harold Offeh—a Ghanaian-born artist who works with many forms of media, including photography and performance—began a series called *Covers*. He looked at the album sleeves of records made by Black artists in the 1970s and '80s, and thought about how the singers were shown on them. How did they stand or sit? Where were they looking? What were they wearing? Why did they want to look like this?

Harold believes album covers are very interesting pieces of visual communication because they do many things. They show the identity of the singer, and they suggest what kinds of songs they sing. They give you an idea of the time and place the records were made. They make you want to buy the records. But what exactly are the covers selling—and how?

To really understand the album covers, Harold began to recreate them by reenacting the poses. But he didn't simply copy the images—he took photographs of himself in different locations, and he performed the poses live to their soundtracks. He also asked other people to get involved, to take their own images. The pictures are so playful and fun, so there was no shortage of volunteers.

In 2017, at Wysing Arts Centre in the U.K., Harold produced an extension of *Covers*—a project called *Lounging*. He had noticed that in the early 1980s there was a trend for Black male singers to recline on their album artwork. It is a pose found in art from ancient times to today.

During the 1980s, there were many new discussions around identity, race, gender and sexuality. Through *Lounging*, Harold questioned what it was like to be a Black man at that time. MTV launched in 1981, and the channel showed very few Black artists to begin with. Since album covers tell stories, make myths, and sell ideas and inspiration, perhaps they were partly a way to show that Black men—and their music—were desirable, too.

The cover of Teddy Pendergrass's *It's Time for Love* album, released in 1981

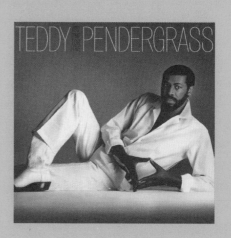

Harold Offeh found that the poses used on many Black male singers' album covers were not comfortable at all—especially on gravel. "Why use these poses?" he asked himself. "Why were they so common?"

LOUNGING

CHRIS OFILI

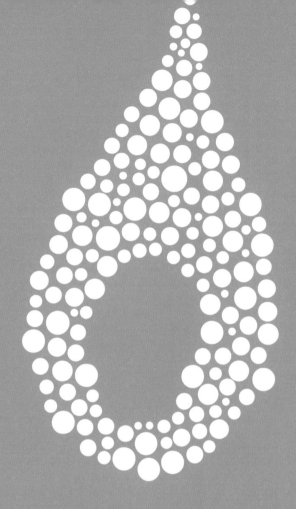

In 1998, artist Chris Ofili made a tribute to Stephen Lawrence, a promising young man who had been murdered in a racist attack in London five years earlier. Stephen had simply been waiting for a bus. *No Woman, No Cry* is the title of Chris's tribute—and it is inspired by Stephen's mother, Doreen. Over the years, Doreen fought tirelessly and courageously to find justice not only for her son, but also for victims of other racist crimes. She founded a trust in Stephen's name, and she worked on reforming how the police work in the U.K.

Watching interviews of Doreen, Chris saw her deep sorrow, but he also recognized the sadness that many people feel, knowing their loved ones will never come home. He understood that grief is, unfortunately, universal.

No Woman, No Cry has the same name as an iconic song, released in 1974, by reggae artist Bob Marley. In that song, Marley gently tells a woman not to be sad. In Chris's work, the woman cries. In each of her tears, if you look closely, are photographs of Stephen Lawrence.

Chris uses many layers and many materials in his mixed-media work. He was once famous for his use of elephant dung, and he used it here. He liked the idea of this earthy material coexisting with the beauty of an art object. Dried and varnished, it is placed on the woman's necklace like a locket. It is also used to give support when the painting of the grieving woman is displayed against a wall. Chris used map pins on these lumps to spell out the title of his work.

NO WOMAN, NO CRY

Chris Ofili's multi-layered artwork is dedicated to Doreen Lawrence, a tireless campaigner for justice. It is also a universal portrayal of sadness and grief.

Chris also used resin, oil, acrylic and a special luminous paint, which you can only really see in the dark. In the right conditions you can read the words "R.I.P. Stephen Lawrence 1974–1993" written across the canvas.

In his song, Bob Marley sings "everything's going to be alright." For a time, it felt that way. Doreen Lawrence's excellent, important work made her well-known and appreciated. In 1998, Chris also became the first Black artist to win the Turner Prize—a significant arts award in the U.K.

However, the Black Lives Matter movement shows us that positive change often begins with the death of Black people—people who will never come home, people who will never benefit from the change they brought to the world.

EMEKA
OGBOH

When Emeka Ogboh first moved from Lagos, Nigeria, to Berlin, Germany, he could not sleep. Not because it was too noisy—quite the opposite. Berlin was too quiet for him. Lagos is never silent, even at night. You might hear an evening congregation, celebrating God at a church. You might hear generators, powering homes and shops. You might hear people at parties, having a great time. To Emeka, this is not simply noise—it is a "sound composition." In an ongoing artwork, he focuses on the particular sounds of the Danfos—yellow minibus-taxis with black stripes— which are symbolic of Lagos.

During the day, Emeka would walk through Lagos with microphones and recording devices capturing honking horns, highway hawkers and hordes of humans. Back in his studio, he would arrange the sounds into audio collages. Rather than just hearing noise, he began actively listening to the layers and details. The city itself made Emeka a "sound artist."

Outside of the Danfo bus in Emeka's installation, you can hear the conductors announcing their routes, like verbal maps. Inside, on headphones, you can hear sounds from the stations—conversations, gossip, people on their phones. You can also listen to music inspired by Emeka's Lagos soundscapes, played on speakers, thanks to the "driver" of the bus. In real life, Danfo bus drivers often play their own music out loud.

LOS-CDG (LAGOS TO PARIS)

Emeka Ogboh's microphones capture the vibrant sounds of Lagos and its iconic yellow Danfo minibus-taxis. Emeka transforms these sounds into art.

Mic and the city, 2014

The Danfo bus itself is clearly a means of transportation—but so are the soundscapes, which immediately transport the listener to the city. Lagos's sounds are so unique that Emeka can always spot them. One time, a friend who lived somewhere else called him on the phone. He wanted to surprise Emeka with a visit. After fifteen seconds of talking, Emeka asked him if he was in Lagos. His friend was shocked that Emeka had guessed where he was right away.

Emeka's work also acts as an archive for Lagos. As the city grows and transforms, the sounds change too. On its new roads, street sellers are now banned; and as official bus routes are expanded, the Danfo taxis will disappear, along with the verbal maps created by their drivers.

TOYIN OJIH ODUTOLA

Toyin Ojih Odutola has moved many times. She lives in New York, but was born in Ife in Nigeria. When she was five, she moved many miles to Berkeley, in California. After four years, her family moved again, this time to Huntsville in Alabama. Her mother, noticing that Toyin was anxious, bought her a *Lion King* coloring book to cheer her up. Toyin loved it—especially Timon, the meerkat. With her pen, she drew him everywhere. As the family drove across the country to their new home, Timon turned up on napkins and notebooks. On that journey, art became Toyin's focus, and the simple ballpoint pen became her tool of choice.

Maebel, from 2012, is a character Toyin created with a pen, a marker and paint. It shows a cropped view of a woman's head and shoulders against a white background. Her skin, "black on black on black"— a description Toyin used—is like a sinewy map of the stars. Its texture is unique and dense. To achieve this, Toyin layers black lines, pressing down hard on the paper. She wants the marks she is making to remain, like an engraving. Depending on the way light bounces off the inky surface, the darkest areas can become the lightest. Toyin sees skin as a landscape, and she wants the viewer to travel through it, discovering her characters.

Pens are also, of course, associated with writers—and Toyin tells stories with her drawings. Her textures and marks are a form of language. She is writing to people, telling them to look and see the depth of Black people.

Since *Maebel*, Toyin has included other materials in her work—dark charcoals and pastel chalks. She has also zoomed out of faces and now features whole bodies in her drawings. Her storytelling power has expanded, too. Toyin's 2018 exhibition, *Testing the Name*, told an imagined story of two wealthy and important families in Nigeria joined together by the marriage of two men— an act that is currently illegal there. Working like a writer, Toyin can spend months inventing fictional narratives in her drawings. Each artwork is like a chapter or an episode, and her audience is invited to weave the story together.

MAEBEL

Pens are often associated with comics and graphic novels—forms that inspire Toyin Ojih Odutola—but she took her passion for the pen to fine art, and created a new way that Black skin could be shown.

ZIZIPHO POSWA

Zizipho Poswa is a South African ceramicist, but she didn't start her career in ceramics. She was a textile designer first, hand-painting colorful patterns onto fabrics. She picked this path intentionally. Zizipho knew that her training would be transferable—and indeed she found her skills were fully suitable for working with clay.

This pair of sculptures—*Ukukhula I* (radiant red, with small scraps of clay from Zizipho's studio) and *Ukukhula II* (bright blue, with flashes of red and spiky triangles)—are both over three feet tall. "Ukukhula" is an iXhosa word that means "growth," but this does not just refer to the sculptures' large size.

Zizipho had been working hard, developing her skills and strengths as an artist. She wanted to create work that showed the stresses and the successes of that journey—the tough times, when she would not give up, but also the positive moments, like her graduation from college.

Ukukhula I and *II*, made in 2018, tell the story of Zizipho's growth in the art world—and her reputation is rising rapidly. These were only the fifth and sixth big sculptures she had made under her own name, but they were quickly bought by the Los Angeles County Museum of Art.

Alongside being a fine artist, Zizipho runs a ceramic studio in Cape Town, which she started in 2006 with another acclaimed artist, Andile Dyalvane. Called Imiso, which means "tomorrow" in English, the studio includes a gallery and a production space. There, the pair run masterclasses and host workshops to inspire the next generation of ceramicists.

These two sculptures are like non-identical twins—from the same family, but different. For Zizipho Poswa, they also play with ideas that seem like opposites but are connected: femininity and masculinity, protection and aggression, the traditional and the new.

FAITH RINGGOLD

In the 1930s, when Faith Ringgold was a small child,
she would visit the Tar Beach—the asphalt roof on the
top of her apartment building in Harlem. On sticky summer
nights, Faith and her siblings would lie on blankets, snack
and stare at the stars. Her parents, and other adults,
would talk and play cards. Faith would look at the George
Washington Bridge, connecting New York to New Jersey.
She would wonder what it would be like to fly over
that bridge, to soar in the sky, to be free.

Faith was interested in art in those early days, and she began her career as a painter. She mostly created still life pictures of plants. But then, in the 1950s and '60s, the civil rights movement began to grow. Faith decided to make work that was important and relevant to her as a Black woman, and that also reflected the turbulent—but ultimately hopeful—world around her. She became an activist and produced political paintings. She taught in schools. She created sculptures and masks, and developed performances for them. She traveled to Europe and Africa.

Faith found that all of her expertise and experience led her to making quilts and adding words to them. This is the art form that she is now most famous for. Sewing was an activity Faith had watched her mother do—back in those childhood days, when she would visit her Tar Beach.

Tar Beach, made in 1988, is the first quilt in Faith's *Women on a Bridge* series. She later turned this quilt's story into a children's book, and wrote many more. In this tale, we follow the fantastic dreams of Cassie Louise Lightfoot, who, on a sticky summer night on a Tar Beach in Harlem, flies over the George Washington Bridge. Cassie proudly says "only eight years old and in the third grade and I can fly. That means I am free to go wherever I want to for the rest of my life."

Faith Ringgold wanted the freedom to tell her story. Through the medium of quilts—a traditional African American craft—her young Black heroine was able to fly high, and feel that the city and the world were hers.

TAR BEACH

ATHI-PATRA RUGA

Athi-Patra Ruga is a South African artist, who often tells mythical stories in his work. In 2013, he made *The Night of the Long Knives I*. There is more to this big, bright image than you might think at first. It is part of a series called *Future White Women of Azania*. Azania is a name that was given to southern and eastern areas of Africa in Ancient Greek and Roman times. The name was used again in the 1960s to describe a perfect South Africa that might exist in the future.

THE NIGHT OF THE LONG KNIVES I

In his rainbow-colored artwork, Athi-Patra Ruga creates his idea of
a utopia—a perfect world—filled with intriguing mythical characters.

By using the name "Azania," Athi-Patra is thinking about Africa as it was before Europeans invaded. He is also thinking about a future Africa, now that apartheid—the era when white and non-white South Africans were separated by race—has ended. In *The Night of the Long Knives I*, he creates his own "Azania," full of fictional characters.

On the left of his photograph are two faceless figures, the *abo dade*. These are sisters who can have children without men—they just have to think about it and they can make babies. On the right is the "Flower of Azania." She is wearing a costume made out of 250 sunhats. In the middle, covered in balloons, is Athi-Patra's "Future White Woman of Azania." She is sitting on a zebra, which is decorated like a Spanish horse or an Indian holy cow.

Athi-Patra wanted his image to have the fanfare and splendor that some special funerals have. He got wreaths from Cape Town, complete with fake flowers, which he and his team sewed onto nets. The fabric he used for the background reminded him of both a garden and a galaxy.

It is a beautiful and fun image, but when thought about in relation to its title, it becomes more serious. During apartheid, a false idea was spread, which people called "The Night of the Long Knives." This idea claimed that when Nelson Mandela died (he was the first Black president of South Africa, who had previously spent 27 years in prison), Black people would violently riot. This never happened. Instead of the promised panic, Athi-Patra pictures a scene of hope and happiness.

AMY
SHERALD

Amy Sherald is an African American painter, who lives and works in Baltimore. She is well known for using the color gray to depict the skin of her subjects. She obtains her signature gray by mixing Mars black and Naples yellow paints together. In 2018, Amy made a painting that became extremely famous. You might recognize the woman in the painting. It is a very important work, because it represents a significant number of "firsts."

Amy was the first African American woman to be commissioned to create a presidential portrait—a tradition that began back in 1797. The woman in her painting—Michelle Obama—is a lawyer and a writer. Her husband was the 44th president of the United States, and so she became the first African American First Lady. Obama herself selected Amy to paint the portrait, saying she was "blown away by the boldness of her colors."

Amy's use of colors is significant. By using gray—a technique called "grisaille"—she is able to remove associations related to race and Black skin, allowing the viewer to just look at the person. Amy's use of grisaille was inspired by looking at black-and-white photographs of her grandmother.

Obama is pictured sitting against a timeless, blue-sky background, and her triangular dress turns her into a monumental mountain. Some people think the dress, with its colored shapes, looks like the brilliant and bold quilts made by descendants of enslaved Africans in Gee's Bend, Alabama.

Amy's painting was hung in the Smithsonian in Washington, but quickly had to be moved to a bigger room because so many visitors came to see it. A photograph of two-year-old Parker Curry, standing in awe at Amy's work, went viral. Obama met Parker, whose mother said afterwards that Parker believed "Michelle Obama is a queen, and she wants to be a queen as well."

Amy Sherald wants to inspire people with her portraits of confident sitters. This painting did just that.

FIRST LADY MICHELLE OBAMA

YINKA SHONIBARE

When Yinka Shonibare was a student, a teacher asked him why he didn't make "authentic African art." Yinka wondered what "authentic" really meant for him. Yinka is connected to both Europe and Africa. He was born in London, and moved to Lagos in Nigeria when he was three. He came back to England to study when he was a teenager. He can speak Yoruba and English. He is interested in the relationship between the two continents, both personally and historically, and he often returns to it in his work.

Butterfly Kid (Girl) IV, made in 2017, is a sculpture of a child. Her finger is pointed as she gently steps forward. Her head is a black globe, inscribed with a map of the night sky—but the stars are named after butterflies. Bright wings on her back, she wears colorful shoes, tights and a bold dress. This is made from Ankara fabric, which Yinka buys from a market in London. People often think of this fabric as a symbol of African identity, but its history is complex.

Ankara fabric was first made in nineteenth-century Europe, but its designs were based on batik patterns from Indonesia. It was then sold in West Africa. These fabrics are now made and exported from Manchester in England and Helmond in the Netherlands. For Yinka, this precisely demonstrates the global connections that he is so interested in.

In this work, Yinka is also looking beyond our world, and into the future. This series of sculptures is partly inspired by the devastating effects of climate change on nature—and how we might escape from it. If we can no longer live on Earth, then perhaps, like the Butterfly Kids, we may be able to grow wings and fly away.

BUTTERFLY KID (GIRL) IV

Yinka Shonibare says his sculptures are "part Victorian, part African, part Dutch." The old-fashioned clothes they wear remind us of the Victorian era. This was the time when Britain colonized and exploited many parts of Africa.

CARRIE
MAE WEEMS

In 1989, Carrie Mae Weems was teaching photography in Massachusetts. Before or after work—whenever she found time—she would set up her camera at one end of her wooden kitchen table. At the other end, she would perform, taking photographs of herself—and often people from her neighborhood—lit only by the hanging lamp above.

Carrie worked on her photographs every day for months. In 1990, she put twenty of her images together to form *The Kitchen Table Series*—a timeless and important body of work that Carrie is now celebrated for. These images are displayed with fourteen pieces of text that tell the story of a 38-year-old woman who has "varied talents, hard laughter, [and] multiple opinions."

In the series, Carrie is the star of snapshots taken from a fictional life. There are images with her and a male partner—both in and out of love. There are images of her with friends and family. There are images of her alone. Through the photographs, Carrie questions ideas about women's roles and traditions. She does this in a kitchen— the space in a house that has historically "belonged" to women.

In the image shown here, a mother and her daughter apply makeup, looking in matching mirrors. They are getting ready at home, in private, presumably to go out in public. The girl is clearly learning from the woman, but what is the lesson? How to be pretty? How to be a woman? In this image, Carrie asks questions about what women share with each other, why, and for whom. Her *Kitchen Table Series* has gone on to inspire many artists, including Black female artists who could see themselves represented in the work, and also on gallery walls.

Carrie Mae Weems's complex and carefully thought-through *Kitchen Table Series* shows the power of storytelling, and how performed images can look and feel so real.

UNTITLED

KEHINDE
WILEY

When Kehinde Wiley was a child, growing up in Los Angeles, he would visit museums and galleries on the weekends. He was intrigued by the large portraits of rich white people— their powdered wigs, their pearls, the puppies sitting proudly in their laps. He was fascinated by how these paintings demonstrated the power of the people in them. He began questioning how Black people could appear in art like this, and how they could fit in with the specific way a "hero" is depicted in such paintings.

Napoleon Leading the Army Over the Alps, created by Kehinde in 2005, is an equestrian portrait—a painting of a person on a horse. These were typically created in the past of important men as a way to assert their dominance. Paintings like these are early examples of "branding"—and they worked very well. For centuries, images like these promoted power. The painting Kehinde's work is inspired by did exactly that.

Kehinde's portrait is based on *Napoleon Crossing the Alps at the Great Saint Bernard Pass*, painted in around 1800 by the French painter Jacques-Louis David (see page 126). Though both titles relate to the great French leader Napoleon Bonaparte, and both reference the Alps mountains, there are key differences between the two paintings.

The composition is nearly identical—both men in the paintings are seated on white horses, and pointing their fingers upward—but Kehinde's painting features a young Black man. Where David's Napoleon wears a general's uniform, a bicorne hat, long leather boots and a gauntlet, Kehinde's Napoleon wears camouflage fatigues, a bandana, Timberland boots and a wristband. The backgrounds are also different: in David's painting the French army are climbing a mountain, but in Kehinde's painting the background is a red and gold tapestry. Kehinde's gold picture frame is also part of his work, and he has included a self-portrait right in the middle, at the top.

NAPOLEON LEADING
THE ARMY OVER THE ALPS

Jacques-Louis David, *Napoleon Crossing the Alps at the Great Saint Bernard Pass*, late 18th–early 19th century

We can find out a lot about Napoleon from books or the internet, but we don't know much about the person in Kehinde's painting—and it's likely Kehinde didn't know much about him at first either. Kehinde walks around cities to find his sitters—he calls this "street casting." The lucky ones who say yes to his invitation get to understand his approach. Back at the studio, they look through books of historical paintings. Some sitters even get the chance to choose which pose they would like to recreate.

Kehinde's close imitation of David's painting—and the way he has carefully chosen which changes to make—shows that he is intrigued by how these historical paintings functioned. In creating his work, he also makes clear that the need for Black people to be visible in the world of art, and to be taken seriously, is of utmost importance to him.

Jacques-Louis David wrote the last name of his subject, "BONAPARTE," on a rock in the foreground of his painting, along with the names of other military commanders who led troops across the Alps. Kehinde Wiley, in his magnificent version, records the last name of his own sitter, "WILLIAMS."

LYNETTE YIADOM-BOAKYE

Lynette Yiadom-Boakye is a British painter, who works in a very interesting way. If you look at a work such as *A Concentration*, which she painted in 2018, you might think she had actually visited a ballet studio and studied the dancers. But she didn't. Her characters are fictional people. She calls them "figments." There are always "people" in Lynette's work, but they are not portraits. She works from her imagination, and from images she has found, in order to create characters for her canvas.

Lynette's picture titles are often very poetic, and this isn't surprising because she is also a writer. "I write about the things I can't paint," she once said, "and paint the things I can't write about."

When she begins a new piece, Lynette knows roughly what she wants to see, and then lets her paints guide her work. That's where her focus is—not on representation of real people, but on the process of painting.

Her process is quite unusual, as she works very quickly. She used to produce a painting in a day—not only because she says she's impatient, but also because she finds it harder to come back to her work when the paint is dry.

Most of the figments in Lynette's paintings share similarities. The people pictured wear simple clothes and are set against simple backgrounds. They don't tend to wear shoes, because shoes make you think of a specific time or place. In addition, Lynette's figments are Black.

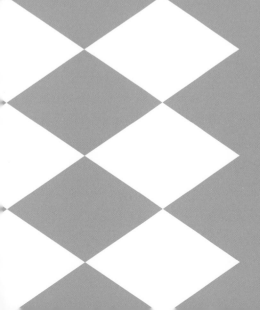

A CONCENTRATION

Lynette Yiadom-Boakye's art features Black people, but this
is not a protest or a celebration. As a Black person herself,
Lynette's blackness is not something *different* or *special*; it just *is*.

GLOSSARY

acrylic – a type of paint that is fast-drying and has been widely used by artists since the 1960s

activist artist – an artist who is actively engaged in addressing social or political issues through their work

apartheid – a system devised by white rulers to separate white people from non-white people ("apartheid" is an Afrikaans word, meaning "apartness"); based on white supremacy (the idea that white people are central to, are superior to and should dominate non-white people), it lasted in South Africa from 1948 to 1994; segregation, in the U.S., was a similar idea, also discriminating against non-white people

archive – a historical record of information about a place or person

artist-in-residence – an artist who has been given the opportunity to live and/or work in a particular place, outside of their usual environment, so they can research or produce artwork

branding – a form of "advertising" that announces high value (most commonly of a product or company)

c. – short for "circa," which is Latin for "around"; if a painting was made c. 1997, that means it was painted in approximately the year 1997

canvas – a surface for painting on; usually a specially prepared piece of cloth that has been stretched tightly over a frame

ceramicist – an artist who works with clay

charcoal – a stick of charred wood that can be used for drawing

civil rights movement – a mass protest begun in the 1950s, carried out by people trying to obtain equality and justice for African Americans

collage – the technique of using different individual elements to create a single image or artwork; the finished work is also called a collage

commission – a special request for an artist to make an artwork, or several artworks, for a particular purpose

composition – the careful arrangement of different elements within an artwork

cropped – an image that has been tightly framed, so that the focus is very specific

diaspora – a term used for people who live outside their ancestral homelands; in many cases, this migration was forced upon them or their ancestors

DSLR – a type of digital camera; the initials stand for "digital single-lens reflex"

engraving – the technique of using a tool to scratch a drawing into a metal plate, after which the plate is printed with ink; the finished work is also called an engraving

equestrian portrait – a picture of a person on a horse; an equestrian statue would be a sculpture of a person on a horse

fine art – works such as paintings, sculptures, photographs and drawings that are not made for a practical purpose or for commercial use such as advertising

foreground – the front part of a picture (as opposed to the background)

gender – the identity, usually expressed as male or female, given to a person at birth

grisaille – the technique of making an artwork entirely in shades of a neutral color like gray; the finished work is also called a grisaille

group show – an exhibition that features the work of more than one artist

installation – a three-dimensional work of art, often large and often designed for a specific space

LGBTQIA+ – a term used for non-heterosexual identity; the initials stand for "lesbian, gay, bisexual, transgender, queer, intersex and asexual," and the plus symbol means there are more terms that can be added to this list

life-size – an artwork that is the actual size of a person or object in real life

marginalized – a term used for any group of people who are regarded as unimportant and not worthy of inclusion in society

media – forms of mass-communication, such as television, newspapers and the internet

medium – the material used to make an artwork, such as paint, wood, bronze, or else the type of art form used to make an artwork, such as painting, sculpture, photography; the plural of "medium" is "media"

mixed-media – a term used for an artwork that is made from a combination of different materials

movement (art) – a group of artists who share interests and ideas that influence the type of art they make

multimedia – a term used for an artwork that is made from a combination of different materials, including an electronic element such as video or audio

oil – a type of slow-drying paint that was widely used by artists in the past, and is still used today

Old Master – an art-history term that describes great European painters working before the year 1800

ongoing work – an artwork that the artist continues to work on for an extended period of time, often using fresh materials to create new forms of the artwork, but following the same theme

Pan-African – a term that unites together all African countries or peoples

performance – an artwork that consists of pre-planned or spontaneous actions, carried out by the artist or by participants

portrait – a picture or sculpture of a person, who is usually real rather than imaginary

practice – the way an artist makes their work; this can mean the type of art they make, the way they think about their art-making, or the physical activity of their art-making

race – a categorization of humans, usually based on shared physical characteristics such as skin color

racism – discrimination against a person or people of a certain categorization, often based on their skin color

resin – a material that can either be natural (derived from plants or insects) or synthetic (manufactured industrially); it is sometimes used to make artworks such as sculptures

score – music or sound composed for a particular purpose, such as an artwork or film

sculpture – a three-dimensional work of art, often—but not always—carved in a material such as marble, bronze or wood

self-portrait – a portrait that an artist makes of themselves

series – several artworks that belong in the same grouping, often sharing the same subject matter

sitter – a person who poses for a portrait

sketch – a quick drawing; artists often make rough sketches before starting on the final version of an artwork

solo show – an exhibition that features the work of one artist

soundscape – musical or non-musical sounds that create an atmosphere or a sense of a particular place

soundtrack – a recording of music or sound

stereotype – a fixed idea about what someone or something is like, often rooted in prejudice

still life – an artwork that depicts an arrangement of objects that do not move, such as vases of flowers or bowls of fruit

studio – the place where an artist works

texture – the look and feel of an artwork, such as rough or smooth

title – the name an artist gives to an artwork they have made

LIST OF ILLUSTRATIONS

Page 43
Lubaina Himid
Figure from *Naming the Money*, 2004. Courtesy the
artist and Hollybush Gardens, London. Photo Andy Keate

Page 44
Kamala Ibrahim Ishag
b. 1939, Sudanese
Photo Mohamed Noureldin, Khartoum, 2019

Page 47
Kamala Ibrahim Ishag
Two Women (Eve and Eve), 2016. Oil on canvas,
190 × 205 cm (74⅞ × 80¾ in.). Courtesy the artist

Page 48
Rosemary Karuga
b. 1928, Kenyan; d. 2021
Photo Nation Media Group PLC

Page 51
Rosemary Karuga
Woman Standing, c. 1997. Collage on paper,
40 × 30 cm (15¾ × 11⅞ in.). Red Hill Art Gallery,
Nairobi. Courtesy the artist's estate

Page 52
Abdoulaye Konaté
b. 1953, Malian
Photo courtesy the artist and Primo Marella Gallery

Page 55
Abdoulaye Konaté
Femme du Sahel, 2015. Textile, 218 × 147 cm (85⅞ ×
57⅞ in.). Courtesy the artist and Primo Marella Gallery

Page 56
Ibrahim Mahama
b. 1987, Ghanaian
Photo Thomas Lohnes/Getty Images

Page 58–59
Ibrahim Mahama
Non-Orientable Nkansa, 2017. Mixed media, dimensions
variable. Photo George Darrell. Courtesy White Cube.
© the artist

Page 60
Ibrahim Mahama
Detail of *Non-Orientable Nkansa*, 2017. Photo George
Darrell. Courtesy White Cube. © the artist

Page 62
Kerry James Marshall
b. 1955, American
Photo © Whitten Sabbatini/New York Times/
Redux/eyevine

Page 64–65
Kerry James Marshall
School of Beauty, School of Culture, 2012. Acrylic
and glitter on unstretched canvas, 274.3 × 401.3 cm
(108 × 158 in.). Birmingham Museum of Art, Birmingham,
AL. Museum purchase with funds provided by Elizabeth
(Bibby) Smith, the Collectors Circle for Contemporary Art,
Jane Comer, the Sankofa Society, and general acquisition
funds (2012.57). © Kerry James Marshall. Courtesy
the artist and Jack Shainman Gallery, New York

Page 66
Hans Holbein the Younger
*Jean de Dinteville and Georges de Selve
("The Ambassadors")*, 1533. Oil on oak, 207 × 209.5 cm
(81½ × 82½ in.). National Gallery, London

Page 68
Zanele Muholi
b. 1972, South African
Photo Jared Siskin/Patrick McMullan via Getty Images

Page 71
Zanele Muholi
Bester I, Mayotte (Hail the Dark Lioness), 2015 from the
series "Somnyama Ngonyama, Hail the Dark Lioness,"
2012–ongoing. Gelatin silver print, 100 × 72 cm
(30 × 28 in.). Stedelijkmuseum, Amsterdam.
© Zanele Muholi. Courtesy Stevenson, Cape Town/
Johannesburg, and Yancey Richardson, New York

Page 72
Magdalene A. N. Odundo DBE, OBE
b. 1950, Kenyan/British
Photo Sophie Green

Page 75
Magdalene A. N. Odundo DBE, OBE
Untitled #15, 1994. Burnished and carbonized terracotta,
45 × 30.4 cm (17½ × 12 in.). Collection the Nelson-Atkins
Museum of Art, Kansas City, MO. Acquired through the
generosity of Morton & Estelle Sosland. © Magdalene
A. N. Odundo DBE, OBE. Photo Assassi Productions '95

Page 76
Harold Offeh
b. 1977, British Ghanaian
Photo Emile Holba

Page 110
Amy Sherald
b. 1973, American
Photo Matt McClain/The Washington Post via Getty Images

Page 113
Amy Sherald
First Lady Michelle Obama, 2018. Oil on linen, 183.2 × 152.7 cm (72⅛ × 60⅛ in.). National Portrait Gallery, Smithsonian Institution; gift of Kate Capshaw and Steven Spielberg; Judith Kern and Kent Whealy; Tommie L. Pegues and Donald A. Capoccia; Clarence, DeLoise, and Brenda Gaines; Jonathan and Nancy Lee Kemper; The Stoneridge Fund of Amy and Marc Meadows; Robert E. Meyerhoff and Rheda Becker; Catherine and Michael Podell; Mark and Cindy Aron; Lyndon J. Barrois and Janine Sherman Barrois; The Honorable John and Louise Bryson; Paul and Rose Carter; Bob and Jane Clark; Lisa R. Davis; Shirley Ross Davis and Family; Alan and Lois Fern; Conrad and Constance Hipkins; Sharon and John Hoffman; Audrey M. Irmas; John Legend and Chrissy Teigen; Eileen Harris Norton; Helen Hilton Raiser; Philip and Elizabeth Ryan; Roselyne Chroman Swig; Josef Vascovitz and Lisa Goodman; Eileen Baird; Dennis and Joyce Black Family Charitable Foundation; Shelley Brazier; Aryn Drake-Lee; Andy and Teri Goodman; Randi Charno Levine and Jeffrey E. Levine; Fred M. Levin and Nancy Livingston, The Shenson Foundation; Monique Meloche Gallery, Chicago; Arthur Lewis and Hau Nguyen; Sara and John Schram; Alyssa Taubman and Robert Rothman. © National Portrait Gallery, Smithsonian Institution

Page 114
Yinka Shonibare CBE
b. 1962, British Nigerian
Photo Karwai Tang/WireImage/Getty Images

Page 117
Yinka Shonibare CBE
Butterfly Kid (Girl) IV, 2017. Fibreglass mannequin, Dutch wax printed cotton textile, silk, metal, globe and steel baseplate, 125 × 79 × 95 cm (49¼ × 31⅛ × 37½ in.). © Yinka Shonibare CBE. All Rights Reserved, DACS/Artimage 2021. Image courtesy Goodman Gallery, Johannesburg. Photo Stephen White & Co.

Page 118
Carrie Mae Weems
b. 1953, American
Photo © Rolex/Audoin Desforges

Page 121
Carrie Mae Weems
The Kitchen Table Series: Untitled (Woman and Daughter with Makeup), 1990. Gelatin silver print, 69.2 × 69.2 (27¼ × 27¼ in.). © Carrie Mae Weems. Courtesy the artist and Jack Shainman Gallery, New York

Page 122
Kehinde Wiley
b. 1977, American
Photo Dimitrios Kambouris/Getty Images

Page 125
Kehinde Wiley
Napoleon Leading the Army Over the Alps, 2005. Oil on canvas, 274.3 × 274.3 cm (108 × 108 in.). Brooklyn Museum, New York. Partial gift of Suzi and Andrew Booke Cohen in memory of Ilene R. Booke and in honor of Arnold L. Lehman, Mary Smith Dorward Fund, and William K. Jacobs, Jr. Fund (2015.53). © 2005 Kehinde Wiley. Used by permission

Page 126
Jacques-Louis David
Napoleon Crossing the Alps at the Great Saint Bernard Pass, late 18th–early 19th century. Oil on canvas, 259 × 221 cm (102 × 87⅛ in.). Châteaux de Malmaison et Bois-Préau, Rueil-Malmaison, France. Photo RMN-Grand Palais (musée des châteaux de Malmaison et de Bois-Préau)/Franck Raux

Page 128
Lynette Yiadom-Boakye
b. 1977, British
Photo David M. Benett/Dave Benett/Getty Images

Page 131
Lynette Yiadom-Boakye
A Concentration, 2018. Oil on linen, 200.3 × 250.2 cm (78⅞ × 98½ in.). © Lynette Yiadom-Boakye. Courtesy the artist, Jack Shainman Gallery, New York, and Corvi-Mora, London

Some of the artists in this book like to include honors next to their name.
CBE: Commander of the Order of the British Empire; Yinka Shonibare received a CBE for his services to art, as did Lubaina Himid and Chris Ofili.
DBE: Dame Commander of the Order of the British Empire; Magdalene Odundo was made a Dame for her services to art and arts education.
OBE: Officer of the Order of the British Empire; Magdalene Odundo received an OBE for her services to art, as did Sonia Boyce.
RA: an elected member of London's Royal Academy of Arts; Yinka Shonibare is a Royal Academician, as are Sonia Boyce and Lubaina Himid; Honorary Royal Academicians, who are from outside the UK, include El Anatsui.

BIBLIOGRAPHY

I read and watched lots of books, articles and films to help me write *Black Artists Shaping the World*. If I listed them all, this book would be twice as big. Instead, here's a small selection. If you want to find out more about the art and artists on the internet, make sure you check with an adult. The text on the websites is not specifically written for young people, but you should be able to see many more images of the artists' work.

Larry Achiampong – https://www.larryachiampong.co.uk/
El Anatsui – https://elanatsui.art/
Sonia Boyce – https://www.royalacademy.org.uk/art-artists/name/sonia-boyce-ra
María Magdalena Campos-Pons – https://www.vanderbilt.edu/arts/maria-magdalena-campos-pons/
Nick Cave – https://nickcaveart.com/
Joana Choumali – https://joanachoumali.com/
Lubaina Himid – http://lubainahimid.uk
Kamala Ibrahim Ishag – https://princeclausfund.org/laureate/kamala-ibrahim-ishag
Rosemary Karuga – http://www.redhillartgallery.com/rosemary-karuga.html
Abdoulaye Konaté – https://www.primomarellagallery.com/en/artists/1/abdoulaye-konate/
Ibrahim Mahama – https://whitecube.com/artists/artist/ibrahim_mahama
Kerry James Marshall – https://jackshainman.com/artists/kerry_james_marshall
Zanele Muholi – https://www.yanceyrichardson.com/artists/zanele-muholi
Magdalene Odundo – https://anthonyslayter-ralph.com/magdalene-odundo
Harold Offeh – https://www.haroldoffeh.com/
Chris Ofili – https://www.victoria-miro.com/artists/6-chris-ofili/
Emeka Ogboh – https://imanefares.com/en/artistes/emeka-ogboh/
Toyin Ojih Odutola – https://toyinojihodutola.com/
Zizipho Poswa – https://www.imisoceramics.co.za/zizipho-poswa.html
Faith Ringgold – https://www.faithringgold.com/
Athi-Patra Ruga – https://zeitzmocaa.museum/artists/athi-patra-ruga/
Amy Sherald – http://www.amysherald.com/
Yinka Shonibare – http://yinkashonibare.com/
Carrie Mae Weems – http://carriemaeweems.net/
Kehinde Wiley – https://kehindewiley.com/
Lynette Yiadom-Boakye – https://jackshainman.com/artists/lynette_yiadom_boakye

Drew, Kimberly. *This Is What I Know About Art* (Pocket Change Collective). New York: Penguin Workshop, 2020.
Drew, Kimberly, and Wortham, Jenna (eds). *Black Futures*. New York: One World Books, 2020.
Godfrey, Mark, and Whitley, Zoé (eds). *Soul of a Nation: Art in the Age of Black Power*. New York: Distributed Art Publishers, 2017.
Lambert, James, with Jackson, Sharna. *Tate Kids British Art Activity Book*. London: Tate Publishing, 2014.
Muholi, Zanele. *Zanele Muholi: Somnyama Ngonyama, Hail the Dark Lioness*. New York: Aperture, 2018.
Powell, Richard, J. *Black Art: A Cultural History* (World of Art). London: Thames & Hudson, 2003.
Ringgold, Faith. *Tar Beach*. New York: Random House, 1997.
Ringgold, Faith. *We Flew Over the Bridge: The Memoirs of Faith Ringgold*. Durham, NC: Duke University Press, 2005.
Sargent, Antwaun (ed.). *Young, Gifted and Black: A New Generation of Artists: The Lumpkin-Boccuzzi Family Collection of Contemporary Art*. New York: Distributed Art Publishers, 2020.

ABOUT THE AUTHOR

Sharna Jackson is an award-winning author and curator who specializes in developing and delivering socially engaged initiatives for children and young people across culture, publishing and entertainment. She was recently the Artistic Director at Site Gallery, an international contemporary art space in Sheffield, U.K., and was formerly the editor of the BAFTA-nominated Tate Kids website. Sharna's debut novel *High-Rise Mystery* (2019) has received numerous awards and accolades, including the Waterstones Children's Book Prize for the Best Book for Younger Readers 2020, and the *Sunday Times* Book of the Week. Sharna also develops books to encourage participation in the arts; her activity books for Tate won the FILAF award for Best Children's Art Book in 2015. She was the Southbank Centre's 2019–20 Imagine a Story author and, together with bestselling illustrator Dapo Adeola, helped 1,200 London schoolchildren write the middle school novel *London/Londoff*. Sharna lives on a ship in Rotterdam in the Netherlands.

ABOUT THE CONSULTANT

Dr Zoé Whitley is the Director of Chisenhale Gallery in London. She co-curated the landmark exhibition "Soul of a Nation: Art in the Age of Black Power," which toured Tate Modern, London; Crystal Bridges Museum of American Art, Arkansas; Brooklyn Museum, New York; the Broad, Los Angeles, and other U.S. venues between 2017 and 2020. Zoé curated the British Pavilion for the 58th Venice Biennale, and has previously been a Curator at London's Hayward Gallery, Tate Modern, Tate Britain and the V&A, and at the Studio Museum in Harlem, New York. She earned her PhD under the supervision of artist Professor Lubaina Himid. Zoé has contributed texts to numerous publications, and is the author of *The Graphic World of Paul Peter Piech*, as well as the children's art activity book *Meet the Artist: Frank Bowling*.

ACKNOWLEDGMENTS

To all the **artists within our pages**, thank you. Thank you for your work, your talent, your generosity and your permission. Thank you for everything you do; it's crucial, urgent and essential.

This book would have been impossible without **Dr Zoé Whitley**. Zoé, your encyclopedic knowledge and kindness are unmatched. Thank you also to **Harriet Ella Richmond**. Harriet, your comments and notes were so helpful and always made me smile!

Thank you, **Anna Ridley** at Thames & Hudson, for tirelessly supporting and championing this book, for many years. To **Roger Thorp** for his encouragement. To **Jenny Wilson** for making words sing; **Belinda Webster** for incredible design; **Maria Ranauro** for stellar picture research; and **Rachel Heley** for the beautiful book production.

Thank you to **Hellie Ogden**, **Ma'suma Amiri** and **Kirsty Gordon** at Janklow & Nesbit for always taking care of me.

And thank you to **everyone reading**. I wrote this for you.

INDEX

For **all the Black artists** out there, keeping on keeping on.

Black Artists Shaping the World © 2021 Thames & Hudson Ltd, London

Text © 2021 Sharna Jackson

Artwork reproductions see pp. 135–138

Consultancy by Dr Zoé Whitley

Edited by Jenny Wilson
Designed by Belinda Webster

First published in 2021 in the United States of America by
Thames & Hudson Inc., 500 Fifth Avenue, New York, New York 10110

Library of Congress Control Number 2021933976

ISBN 978-0-500-65259-6

Printed and bound in China by C & C Offset Printing Co. Ltd

MIX
Paper from
responsible sources
FSC® C008047

Be the first to know about our new releases, exclusive content and author events by visiting
thamesandhudson.com
thamesandhudsonusa.com
thamesandhudson.com.au

LARRY ACHIAMPONG EL ANATSUI SONIA
NICK CAVE JOANA CHOUMALI LUBAINA HI
ABDOULAYE KONATÉ IBRAHIM MAHAMA
A.N. ODUNDO HAROLD OFFEH CHRIS OFILI
FAITH RINGGOLD ATHI-PATRA RUGA AMY
KEHINDE WILEY LYNETTE YIADOM-BOAKY
MARÍA MAGDALENA CAMPOS-PONS NICK
IBRAHIM ISHAG ROSEMARY KARUGA ABD
MARSHALL ZANELE MUHOLI MAGDALENE
OGBOH TOYIN OJIH ODUTOLA ZIZIPHO POS
SHERALD YINKA SHONIBARE CARRIE MAE
LARRY ACHIAMPONG EL ANATSUI SONIA
NICK CAVE JOANA CHOUMALI LUBAINA HI
ABDOULAYE KONATÉ IBRAHIM MAHAMA
A.N. ODUNDO HAROLD OFFEH CHRIS OFILI
FAITH RINGGOLD ATHI-PATRA RUGA AMY
KEHINDE WILEY LYNETTE YIADOM-BOAKY
MARÍA MAGDALENA CAMPOS-PONS NICK
IBRAHIM ISHAG ROSEMARY KARUGA ABD
MARSHALL ZANELE MUHOLI MAGDALENE
OGBOH TOYIN OJIH ODUTOLA ZIZIPHO POS
SHERALD YINKA SHONIBARE CARRIE MAE